BIRDS OF PREY
OSPREYS

by Mary R. Dunn

Consulting Editor: Gail Saunders-Smith, PhD

Consultant: Jessica Ehrgott, Bird and Mammal
Trainer, Downtown Aquarium, Denver

CAPSTONE PRESS
a capstone imprint

Pebble Plus is published by Capstone Press,
1710 Roe Crest Drive, North Mankato, Minnesota 56003
www.capstonepub.com

Library of Congress Cataloging-in-Publication Data
Dunn, Mary R.
Ospreys / by Mary R. Dunn.
pages cm.—(Pebble Plus. Birds of Prey)
Includes bibliographical references and index.
Summary: "Describes the characteristics, habitat, behavior, life cycle, and
threats to osprey"—Provided by publisher.
Audience: Ages 5–8.
Audience: Grades K to 3.
ISBN 978-1-4914-2091-1 (library binding)
ISBN 978-1-4914-2309-7 (paperback)
ISBN 978-1-4914-2332-5 (eBook PDF)
1. Osprey—Juvenile literature. I. Title.
QL696.F36D86 2014
598.9'3—dc23
2014032769

Editorial Credits
Jeni Wittrock, editor; Peggie Carley and Janet Kusmierski, designers;
Svetlana Zhurkin, media researcher; Katy LaVigne, production specialist

Photo Credits
Shutterstock: Arend Trent, cover, back cover, balounm, back cover (background),
David Byron Keener, 15, dmvphotos, 21, FloridaStock, 19, Guido Bissattini, 9, Kirsten
Wahlquist, 1, Paul Vinten, 17, Stubblefield Photography, 11, Tony Campbell, 13,
Vladimir Kogan Michael, 5, 7

Note to Parents and Teachers

The Birds of Prey set supports national science standards related to
life science. This book describes and illustrates ospreys. The images
support early readers in understanding the text. The repetition of
words and phrases helps early readers learn new words. This book
also introduces early readers to subject-specific vocabulary words,
which are defined in the Glossary section. Early readers may need
assistance to read some words and to use the Table of Contents,
Glossary, Read More, Internet Sites, Critical Thinking with the
Common Core, and Index sections of the book.

Printed in the United States of America in Stevens Point, Wisconsin
102014   008479WZS15

Table of Contents

Flying Fishers

An osprey dives from the
sky into the water. Splash!
It catches a fish with its feet
and flies back to its nest.

Up Close!

Ospreys have brown feathers on their backs. White feathers cover their bellies. An osprey's strong wings spread out about 6 feet (1.8 meters).

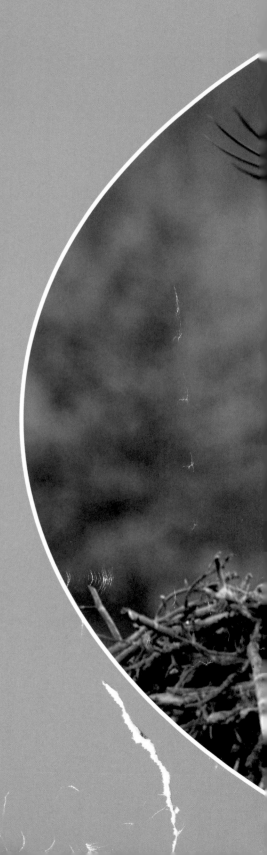

Ospreys have long legs and blue-gray feet. Hook-like talons on their feet help ospreys catch and hold slippery fish.

9

Home Sweet Home

Four kinds of ospreys live around the world. They are on every continent except Antarctica. Some migrate in winter. Others stay in one place.

Osprey Range

where ospreys live

Ospreys build big nests.
They use sticks, leaves,
fur, and grass. Some
nests weigh more than
400 pounds (181 kilograms).

Favorite Food

Ospreys' favorite food is
fresh fish. Sometimes they
snack on birds, snakes,
or squirrels.

Growing Up

Females lay two to four white, spotted eggs. They hatch after six weeks. A nest of chicks eats 7 pounds (3 kg) of fish a day.

Chicks learn to fly in about
two months. They stay with
their parents until they learn to
fish. Wild ospreys usually live
about 20 years.

Keeping Safe

In some states, ospreys are endangered. They cannot find safe places to build nests. Laws were made to protect ospreys and their homes.

Glossary

chick—a young bird

endangered—in danger of dying out

hatch—to break out of an egg

migrate—to move from one place to another

slippery—wet and hard to hold

spotted—marked with small spots

talon—a sharp, curved claw

Read More

Curtis, Jennifer Keats. *Osprey Adventure.* Atglen, Penn.: Schiffer Pub., 2011.

McDowell, Pamela. *Ospreys in Danger.* Orca Echoes. Custer, Wash.: Orca Book Publishers, 2014.

Sill, Catherine. *About Raptors.* About Series. Atlanta: Peachtree Publishers, 2010.

Internet Sites

FactHound offers a safe, fun way to find Internet sites related to this book. All of the sites on FactHound have been researched by our staff.

Here's all you do:

Visit *www.facthound.com*

Type in this code: 9781491420911

 Check out projects, games and lots more at **www.capstonekids.com**

Critical Thinking Using the Common Core

Why do you think some ospreys migrate in winter but other ospreys do not?
(Integration of Knowledge and Ideas)

How do ospreys catch their food?
(Key Ideas and Details)

Index

Word Count: 199
Grade: 1
Early-Intervention Level: 14

24